PONDERINGS

Wellsprings of Country Wisdom

by

KENNETH E. GRANT

The C.R. Gibson Company
Norwalk, Connecticut 06856

DEEP WELL
WATER

It was hotter than all git-out, and I was sitting in the shade of the barn daydreaming. You could see the heat dancing in the road leading to the highway. Out in the pasture, most of the cattle were lying in the shade of the cottonwoods or gathered around the water trough by the windmill. Luckily, there was a little breeze blowing, so that windmill was turning. I knew that meant cool water would be splashing into the trough, and those cows would have their noses down in it. Just thinking about it made me thirsty so I got up and went around to the pump (we still have one of the old kind at our place), took the tin cup that's always hangings there and, after working the handle a few times, saw fresh water come gurgling up and splash into my cup. Reckon city folks can't get water like that, even from those big bottles they pay for!

I went back and sat down and began pondering. I remembered that the Good Book says that those who believe in Jesus will be like a well of water, only the well being inside them and never running dry. On a hot day like that, it sounded like a right practical arrangement!

Then I got thinking about that windmill...and the pump. Jesus didn't mentioned them being necessary for getting at the kind of water He's talking about. Of course I knew He was talking about *spiritual* water. . .and maybe that kind doesn't need pumping. But the more I thought about it, the more I wasn't sure. It appears to me a fellow can run dry in his inner parts very quickly unless he sets about doing something about it. There's where the mill and the pump handle come in.

It appears to me that wind and spirit have things in common. For example: both are invisible but mighty powerful on occasion. I figure that there are times when the Good Lord comes sweeping into our lives and turns the windmill of our souls. We perk up then and just naturally start doing things His way. Love and kindness and good living come welling up from down deep in us and everyone around gets blessed! But there are other times when we have to work the handle and pump awhile before we see any water in our cup. . .or have any to give away. Praying and reading the Good Book, riding to church on a Sunday, being kind and decent even when we don't feel much like it. . .all that's pumping, I figure. Yes, and sometimes we may even need a bit of priming, somebody else pouring a little love and kindness into our lives, before our pump starts working!

Either way, the water will come. It's there, down deep, if we belong to the Almighty. If we have been riding with Jesus for a spell, even when the weather's hotter than the hinges of hell, the spiritual water'll be there. . .and will come. . .if we're willing to pump a bit.

SPIRITUAL STIRRUPS

I remember, back when I was a kid, climbing on a neighboring farmer's wagon horse with only some old scrap wire fastened to the halter for a rein. That patient creature would haul me around the field at a slow walk with me sitting happy-as-a-cricket on that broad back. But I remember, too, the day he broke into a trot, and I went sliding off into a sage bush. It happened so quickly that I didn't have time to grab a handful of mane. Since I was riding bareback, there weren't any stirrups to keep me from sliding. The ground seemed a whole lot farther away in those days...and awful hard!

All that's a way of saying that stirrups are a mighty useful item when it comes to riding a horse. They give a body someplace to plant his feet and keep balanced, especially when a horse takes it into his head to move in some direction you weren't counting on! Stirrups also come in mighty handy when climbing on or getting off a horse. Plain or fancy, stirrups have their place.

It strikes me that all this has a spiritual side. Why, there are just a whole lot of things in our lives that can unseat us unless we've got our feet planted and can keep our balance. Then it's important to have what I suppose you could call "spiritual stirrups."

Now you take Ellen Whippen. She lives with her brother in an apartment just back of the church in town. Ellen's a widow. The same day her husband died there was an accident down at the mill that crippled her brother. It seems it was one thing after another. Yet, somehow, that woman found strength to go on when nobody thought she could.

One day, in the middle of it all, I ran into her walking out along the highway on a Sunday afternoon. We began talking and that's when I learned about Ellen Whippen's stirrups.

"I won't pretend," she said. "It's not easy. Not at all! In fact, I probably wouldn't be able to go on except..." She stopped and looked at me with quiet, blue-grey eyes. "Except for the Almighty," she said. "God has been very close these past months. Do you know what I mean?" "I sure do," I replied. "I've been through spells in my own

life when I'm downright certain I'd never have made it without the Almighty's help." She took a deep breath and sighed. "I'm awful glad you understand," she said. "Somehow I thought you would." Ellen smiled and put her hand on my arm.

"The Lord's the center of my life and has been since I was a little girl. Having faith in Him, why that means more than almost anything!" She paused a moment, looking thoughtful. "But love's important too, both God's love and the love other folks give. A person could hardly live a day without that! I guess it's sort of like having your feet set in spiritual stirrups so that life can't throw you. Faith's got to be one of them and love's the other."

I pondered a good deal about what she'd said as I continued on home. After all, the Good Book does talk about there being three things that don't change with the years: faith, hope, and love. Ellen had mentioned two of them. But what about hope?

When I spotted her at church that next Sunday, I asked her about that. She smiled at me with that big, broad smile. "I know," she said. "I thought about it right after you left. The Good Book puts hope in there right along with faith and love. Of course I have hope! When you know you're loved, and have faith that the Almighty's watching over you, hope just comes naturally, wouldn't you say?"

It took me a time to answer. I took her hand and we stood there a moment in silence. Finally, I cleared my throat and said in a husky voice. "Yes, I believe that's about what I'd say, too."

That plucky little woman had put it about as well as a body could. Faith and love were Ellen Whippen's "spiritual stirrups," both being necessary to keep her in the saddle. And hope was where she sat! She was centered good and proper in the saddle of hope...and could ride out the rough spots because both faith and love kept her hopes alive!

THE WHEAT FIELD

*I*t came to me not long back when my horse threw a shoe. I got off and walked back a hundred yards or so looking for it. 'Happened to look over the fence into the field there by the road where ole man Smith has a stand of summer wheat growing. It looked right promising. Come Fall, it'll be beautiful, waving like a golden ocean in the sunshine!

I got to thinking then about people and wheat, how there's some similarities. Take for example how no two of those heads of wheat are just alike, however much they look it when you're standing back. I guess no two of us are just alike either, though the further back you stand the easier it is to say, "Folks are all pretty much the same." No, they aren't. Not really. The Almighty knows the differences, too, not only between each one of those heads of wheat on its stalk but also between each one of us on our two legs! Yep, and He's made allowances for it in His dealings with us. You can count on that.

It struck me, too, how that field was kind of like the world and all of us folks in it. . .the wind being like the Spirit of God. 'Preacher told me once that Bible folks used to think the two were the same, since both are invisible and still have the power to do great things. Come Fall, the wind'll be moving gentle-like over ole man Smith's field, and it'll be waving like a golden ocean, that ripe wheat bending down in the sunshine as beautiful as can be! And I figure the Spirit of God is moving today over this world of His. And when we're ripe and ready, folks everywhere will bow down before the Son of God...and that'll be beautiful too...because where *that* happens, things just can't help but get a whole lot better.

There's another angle come to mind. Struck me that when the wheat is all gold and bowing down like that, harvest time is not far off. I'm not just sure what that'll mean, but I reckon the Almighty does! I figure the best any hand of His can do is to see to it that he does what's required of him and stays close to Jesus. Harvest'll come around in His good time.

A MATTER OF STYLE

*O*ur foreman came by a minute ago and said, "I don't know what you're thinking but I hope it doesn't hurt...though you'd never know it by looking at your face." I told him I was thinking about folks and their ideas about religion. Some of them sure make a fuss! Others, well, they have another style.

It all started yesterday when I was in town picking up supplies for the ranch. I'd stopped at General Mercantile and couldn't help overhearing some of the town folks talking. Seems one of them was hopping mad at the preacher because he didn't say enough in his sermon last Sunday about sin and how folks are going to hell right and left. A couple of others said they were downright glad he didn't. Said they'd heard that for years and were glad the Parson had something more encouraging to say. At any rate, it was pretty plain nobody was getting convinced and weren't likely to *that* day.

Now the Parson and I have been friends for quite a spell. I remember one day a good many years ago when I was out riding on Shadow Mountain and I came across him walking the trail alone. "Hello, Parson," I said. "You're a good piece from town for a man not on horseback." He allowed how that was so but that he did it regularly so he could be by himself and think things over. "Besides," he said, "it keeps the blood running good and strong." I apologized for bothering him and was going to ride on, but he asked me to walk with him a spell. That seemed neighborly. . . so I did. Before we were through I knew his story and he knew mine. . .and we have been good friends ever since.

Maybe that will explain why I respect that man about as much as any I know. He can't toss a rope and is only middling good on horseback, but when it comes to helping folks, there isn't a better hand around. And I know more than one person in town that's friends with Jesus because the Parson introduced them somewhere along the line. But nobody can accuse him of being pushy! No, sir! He's not one to talk religion when you'd rather talk fishing. Fact is, I suspect he'd sometimes just as soon talk fishing himself. Still, somehow, before you're through, the Almighty has come into the conversation, easy and natural-like, without anybody getting upset. That's just his style.

Of course, as I said, it doesn't suit everybody. Appears as for some folks, religion depends a good deal on words, the *right* words as they see it. They figure a body's got to *talk* religion just right (which is to say, their way) before they consider them part of the Almighty's outfit. But you know, I discovered a long time ago that there are things about love and friendship that are mighty hard to put into words. . .especially when your friend is the Almighty! Still it seems that those who are His friends show it. They show it by a kind of living that marks them as being one of Jesus' hands. And, sooner or later, it'll come into their conversation easy and natural, with nobody getting upset.

I figure that's the style that suits me. It should. After all, that's the way it was that day on Shadow Mountain when the Parson and I got acquainted...and he introduced me to his Boss.

REVEREND BEST

===

I was only a little shaver when I first met him. I suppose that's why the picture is sort of dim...like looking at somebody through an old, lace curtain. Still, the figure of Reverend Best sticks in my mind after all these years...and it's a mighty good memory.

He was born in England. Came to this country as a young man after getting schooled to be a minister of the Gospel. What led him to America a body can only guess. Maybe the same thing that led folks before him—a hankering for adventure and the sight and smell of places he'd never been. At any rate, he finally found his way to Craig, Colorado, sometime early in this century...and there he settled down. Seemed to know that this was where the Almighty wanted him. He stayed the rest of his life.

Craig wasn't much in those days...only two paved roads...the highways which crossed in the center of the town. But the dusty streets were shaded by big cottonwoods and the Yampa River flowed just south of town,

greening up the valley and providing water for stock and crops alike. Craig was pretty much like a thousand other little towns I guess, but it was special for Reverend Best and the folks who called it home.

Among those folks were my Aunt Jane and Uncle Ted. Ted had come to Craig as a 16 year-old orphan boy. Got himself a job with the newspaper and worked hard. Before he was through, he was the best veterinarian in western Colorado as well as being a partner in that newspaper. Aunt Jane kept busy as a cricket writing for the paper and raising their three kids. I used to visit in the summer time, going on vet calls with Uncle Ted, fishing with my cousins in Fortification Creek and putting away my Aunt's good cooking.

I remember Reverend Best coming to dinner of a Sunday afternoon, everybody gussied up and sitting around the big, family table. Reverend Best was guest of honor, but he'd have everybody joshing and laughing before you knew it! His blue eyes sparkled, and the crinkles spread out from the corners when he laughed. I didn't know much about his religion, but I figured something about it must be mighty good to make him and those around him so happy. And happy they surely were. . .in that dusty little town with two paved streets.

Reverend Best always wore a dark suit and one of those preacher's collars with the white notch in front. He was a short, roly-poly, little man, and the thinning hair was turning white. You could still hear a good deal of England in his talk (sounding a mite strange in Craig, Colorado), but there was nothing strange about Reverend Best. He fit the place and the people as if he'd been born there. And maybe, in a sense, he had. Folks loved him. He shared their joys and their sorrows. He married their young and buried their old and gave folks in between lots of encouragement and hope. He was part and parcel of their life.

All that was long ago. Craig is a good deal bigger now, and the streets are long since paved. Aunt Jane and Uncle Ted are buried in the cemetery east of town, along with Reverend Best and most of the other folks I see through that old lace curtain. I can stand now, listening to the wind in the grass, looking down at the markers. . .remembering. And somehow I see the little man in the dark suit smiling and laughing, the crinkles running out from the corners of those sparkling blue eyes. And I reckon I know why a whole town loved him. . .and why they named the new Hall after him at the Church.

When I get to pondering, I know that it ought to be this way with us all. Each of us needs to find that place where our heart is at peace, where we can settle down and love folks in a way that'll make them glad we were born. It may be a far journey from where we started. But then, when the wind whispers over the place where we rest, folks'll know we're finally where we were headed all along, Home on the Master's Spread, glad for the way we've come. . .and the Mighty Hand that led us every step.

YOUNG WILL

I suppose there never was a country boy that didn't get an itch to move to the city at one time or another. I reckon city folks must get the itch to move to the country now and then, too. The ole saying about the grass being greener on the other side of the fence doesn't say where that fence is, but I suspect each of us has found it a time or two. Usually a body'll find they're happiest where their roots go deepest, though it takes some of us a while to find that out.

Take Will Smith's young-un. His folks raised him right. He grew up to be about as fine a hand as any in these parts, with all the girls watching as he walked by because he was good looking to boot. He knew it, too, but it didn't turn his head. He was from good stock, and he showed it.

Then, one day, young Will (he had his daddy's name) came to that fence we were talking about and decided to go adventuring. His folks didn't try to stop him. Guess they knew he had to find his own way. So, the boy packed up and moved to the city and enrolled in college. At first he wrote home regularly but before long, the letters thinned out. His folks didn't mention him much after that. . .just that Will was "away finding out what God had for him."

Now as I said, Will was a smart boy and so nobody was surprised to hear one day how he'd graduated with honors and was doing real well working for some big company, making lots of money and driving a fancy car. It wasn't long before he'd found himself a young woman and married her, the two of them moving into a big house. Looked like young Will had found that green pasture he was looking for beyond the fences of our valley.

Years went by without much word. Then, one day, the news came. Seems that business troubles had hit the company real hard...and they'd let Will go. His wife, used to living in fancy circles, left him when their place had to be sold. Will wrote his folks that he was feeling awful tired and wanted to come home and rest a spell.

That was ten years ago. Seems the minute he stepped off the train and took a deep breath of country air something clicked inside of him. Of course his Ma and Pa were there to greet him too, and it was ole home week at the church supper that night, everybody laughing and slapping him on the back. And the women folk, they were hugging and kissing him as though he were their own kin...which in a sense you had to say he was. Later, at the close of the evening service, Will walked down front during the invitations and knelt, tears streaming down his face. It appears the boy'd come home several ways ...and this was the most important of them all.

Will's got a farm of his own now, not far off. His wife came back, too, not long after. Seems as how, though she was raised a city girl, she fell in love with our valley. Now they're expecting a young-un and everybody's getting ready for the big event!

As I said, folks are usually happiest where their roots go deepest. But geography is only part of it. I figure every one of us needs to be at home with the Almighty in his or her own heart. And when we have tried every side of the fences of this life, that homecoming has got to be the one that counts the most. Ask Will.

HOBBLED

She's an old lady, a "senior",
she'd rather you'd say, and she can't get out of bed. The
hard years she's known have taken their toll on her body
and brought her into her seventies pretty well crippled
up. Now she does all her living in bed, sort of "hobbled"
I guess you'd say, in body if not in spirit.

But that distinction is mighty important. Olga is alive,
more alive than a lot of people I know who have no trouble
getting around. She lives in a little old apartment in town
("vintage," she calls it) but her mind and imagination range
the whole, wide world! She has a good woman, Betty,
who comes in every day to cook and clean and handle
other chores around the place. But Olga keeps herself
busy, I'll tell you! She's always writing poetry, sending
letters or planning little gifts she can send off to folks who
need cheering up.

Olga is a friend of mine, and I'm mighty thankful for
that. I've been dropping in to see her for a good many
years now. When I've something weighing on my mind
and need a friend who'll listen, I drop by to see Olga. She'll
send me to the kitchen to fix a cup of tea and then we'll
talk. Of course she doesn't know beans about ranching
or cows, but shucks, that doesn't matter. She knows a

whole lot about people. It appears she's known some of almost every kind and, most importantly, she's on good speaking terms with the Almighty. That, you can tell, though she doesn't go on about it. You can just tell.

I dropped in one day awhile back when the leaves were beginning to turn and the air had the nip of coming winter about it. Olga welcomed me with a smile that spread clear across her big, round face. "Hello," I said, pulling the door shut behind me to keep out the draft. "What's new?" Right off, I felt a twinge of guilt thinking there wasn't likely to be much new in her world. But I was wrong. "Oh lots!" she said, and proceeded to tell me about the gingerbread cookies she and Betty were baking to send off to a friend in the east, and about the letter from a publisher saying that some of her poems would be published soon. That twinge I'd felt disappeared.

The things I had to say seemed pale beside all that. I told her that the trees along the country lanes were turning shades of red and gold now and that the sky at twilight was soft with pink clouds. I told her about the way things were going at the ranch and how we were getting ready for winter, the horses growing their winter coats and the hands chopping wood for the fireplaces. She listened as she always does, smiling and nodding. "I'd love to see it," she said. "I wish you could," I answered, "but it seems the Almighty sort of has you hobbled here just now."

Her face looked wistful. "I guess so," she said, "but then, there's so much to be thankful for. There's a good deal more on television than there used to be, even out here in the country. Why, I'm lying right here beside a window on the whole, wide world! Of course there's some things I don't much care to see, but I just turn them off. You say I'm hobbled? I'm not so sure. . .I'm not sure at all! Why, you just took me for a lovely ride along a country lane."

We finished our tea, and I headed home. I pondered a good deal as I drove home through the evening twilight, leaving the lights of town behind. It does seem we sometimes get things backwards. Why, Olga isn't the one who's hobbled. It's the folks who've given up on living, folks whose hopes have died and whose minds and imaginations have closed to the world around them. The hobbled of this world are those who have stopped caring about other folks and have lost touch with the Almighty. . .who cares for us all.

BILLY

*H*e was the orneriest kid I ever met. The foreman brought him down to the barn and introduced him saying, "This is Billy, my nephew. I want you to introduce him to ranch life and see if you can't make a good hand of him."

I took one look at Billy and knew I was in for a tussle. That kid had a look in his eye like many a bronc I've seen and steered clear of. He had ideas of his own that had little to do with mine except that they were different. Billy knew nothing about horses or ranching and didn't care to learn, leastwise not from me.

I bucked him for awhile. But, like most strong-willed horses I've known, that only made him more stubborn. I tried to show him how to mount a horse good and proper and how to hold reins and sit back centered in the saddle. But Billy was determined to ignore every instruction. Say it strong, and he bucked. Say it gentle, and he paid no attention.

There was a green-broke, bay colt in the barn that Billy was itching to ride. He was a handsome piece of horse flesh but with fire smoldering in his eye. I told Billy he wasn't ready for him yet. But Billy, true to form, had his own ideas. One day, when I wasn't looking, he saddled that colt for a ride.

I saw them flash past...and one look told me Billy wasn't in charge. They were headed for the highway at a dead run, and I knew I had to do something quick. My mare was ground-tied only a few feet away, so I jumped aboard and took after them.

I never had the chance to overtake them. The bay hit a badger hole and went down...and Billy went flying! When I rode up, he was lying still and white...and the colt had a broken leg.

Billy was in the hospital for a good spell. When they allowed visitors, I went to see him. "Billy," I said, "I reckon you don't need me preaching to you. But maybe it'll help some if you know that I was once a bull-headed kid too ...and climbed on a lot of horses I never should have mounted. We were *both* lucky, you and me."

"The good Lord knows each one of us needs to learn one way or another. He's provided a lot of clear guiding in the Good Book which many folks choose to ignore. . . just as you ignored my telling you about that colt. And it's a sign of His love that He lets us do it our way, knowing that only the experience of getting thrown now and then is likely to teach us better. Somehow we have to learn, the same as a hot-blooded horse. Afraid your colt didn't learn in time."

I saw Billy's eyes puddle then and he swallowed kinda hard.

Billy still made his mistakes. He was born stubborn I reckon. But, as months passed, he gradually simmered down, listened more, and finally turned into a pretty fair hand. 'Matter of fact, he even rides to church every Sunday morning now.

I still ride my chestnut mare, and she has plenty of fire for an old hand. But she's learned her lessons long ago and, come to think of it, so have I. Yet, a fellow can't stop learning while the Lord keeps teaching. And He still does!

WINTER
GRASS

Winter on the range is no fun. . .though it's often beautiful in its own way. But when the snow gets deep and the cattle have trouble digging for grass, a fellow has to keep busy even if the weather is downright miserable and he is, too! Those cows need caring for, and it's a cowpoke's job to do it.

I got to thinking about that not long ago. It struck me that there are times in people's lives when the grass is buried pretty deep. . .and we gotta do a heap of digging just to get by. It's mighty good to know then that the Almighty is riding herd.

It was that way for me years back. The job I had petered out. The outfit I was working for hit hard times, and the hands were leaving one by one. When I took leave, I had no idea where the trail was leading, only that somehow the Almighty was still in charge and would see to it that I was taken care of. That's when I got to thinking about this valley where I'd been raised. . .and headed back.

It was a long trip, and as I rode, I thought of all those years I'd spent knocking around from state to state, doing all sorts of jobs, mostly around ranches and now and then a rodeo or two. Looking back I could see how the Al-

mighty'd stepped in more than once to haul me out of some dangerous spot and lead me to food when I didn't know where the next meal was coming from. I knew then that the Boss'd been riding herd all along...even when I was feeling awfully lost, and the grass was buried pretty deep.

I reckon that's why I keep a copy of the Good Book in my saddle bag now. Of course there isn't always time for reading when work's heavy. But there are other times when the herd is quiet, and there's nothing real pressing to get done. Then I take that book out of my saddle bag and read a page or two, asking as I do for understanding to match my reading. Sometimes it will come clear as day and others it doesn't...but most often I'm a heap better off for reading. I know too, better than I did before I started, that the Almighty's close by, riding herd on this old hand.

As I said, winter on the range isn't easy for man or beast. Storms come up that'll darn near blow your whiskers off! But I have been around long enough to know that come Winter, Summer, Spring, or Fall, the Almighty is riding real close to those who are His own. And I reckon that's just about everyone that wants to be. . .and has let Jesus take charge.

THE FIELD MOUSE
AND THE HAWK

*I*t was one of those days that makes a fellow glad he's alive, sky blue as could be with big bunches of white cloud floating along. It sort of looked like the Almighty'd done His washing and hung those clouds out to dry.

I was sitting in the shade of the cottonwoods eating a bite of lunch and taking all this in when I noticed a red-tail hawk circling way up high, easily and naturally riding on the wind. I figured he must be hungry, too, and looking for his supper down in the meadow. I was so busy watching him that I didn't notice the field mouse scurrying around a few feet away. I'd been sitting so still while watching the red-tail that he'd decided it was safe to come out and go about his business. Of course as soon as I moved my boot, he disappeared in the tall grass. "You'd better watch it little fellow," I said, "or before this day's over, you may be supper for that red-tail sailing up there."

That set me to pondering the ways of the Almighty. Of course, both hawks and mice are His doing. He made them, the same as He made you and me. And I suppose He made me to ride a horse and chase cows, just as He made that hawk to sail the sky and that mouse to spend his life scurrying around our meadow...unless that hawk gets him for supper. But then, that's got to be part of the Almighty's plan. That red-tail's bound to have a nest of young-uns to feed...and mice and other small critters are their natural food. That mouse doesn't see things just that way I reckon...or that hawk either. Both of them just go about doing what the Good Lord made them for. It's just we humans that get to pondering it. I wrapped the last half of my sandwich and put it in my saddle bag for later, thinking as I did how most of those cows down the valley would become supper for city folks before the year was out.

I climbed on my horse then and rode down to the herd which was grazing peacefully. "Lord," I said, almost out loud, "is that the trouble with us, that we just don't understand Your system? Seems like we got enough sense to raise questions but not enough faith to trust You when things get hard and the answers are too big for us to understand. Yet somehow, Boss, You must have it all worked out good and proper. Somehow it must be all right for the red-tail to take that field mouse home to feed his young-uns, just as I reckon it's all right for folks to like good beef...though that'd be a mite hard to accept if you were a field mouse or a steer and could think about it."

"Maybe that's it, Lord," I said. "We can think about it. Now I'm certain You gave us brains for more than filling a hat. You gave us enough good sense to stay out of trouble. . . if only we'd use it. But there are times we don't. And sooner or later we all come up against something we can't handle and there's nothing we can do. . . like the field mouse when he's failed to see the shadow of the hawk. Help us to trust You then, Boss, when things are tougher than all-get-out. Help us remember that beyond the hardest trail we'll ever ride there's a great Home Spread where all Your creatures are safe and happy."

I pushed back my hat and watched the red-tail slide down the mountain air and flatten out into a lazy circle. I thought: "Lord, I don't know how You handle all Your business, but I do know from Jesus that You do it all in a loving way. . . a way that's often too much for a fellow like me to understand."

About that time a young steer took a notion to go adventuring and I had to get busy. Seems there's times for pondering and times for hard riding. One usually comes to an end where the other begins. Seems how. . . that's the system!

THE HIGHWAY

Last spring the meadow alongside the highway was as pretty as any garden in town, wild flowers everywhere. A couple of our milk cows were standing in the middle, chewing their cud in the sunshine. I thought to myself, "Lord I do hope heaven's as downright beautiful as our valley."

Then's when I noticed a fellow walking along the road. He had a bedroll on his back and was staring at the ground as he walked, almost as though he were counting the steps. He looked mighty worn and ragged, everything about him appeared to be the same faded shade of grey. Since I was out by the gate checking the mailbox, I waited

'til he got close and said, "Hello." He didn't say anything, just glanced up and kept walking. Then, he stopped suddenly, looked around with a question on his face, and said: "You live there?" I said "Yup." He said he could use a drink of water. . .and we walked together up toward the ranch house.

Well, he got his drink of water all right, and a good meal besides. And we told him he could bed down with us for a day or two, if need be. That loosened his tongue considerably, and he told us his story. I can't tell it all here, but it wasn't pretty. Seems his Ma and Pa were parted young, and he ran off, trying to find some place that needed or wanted him. He didn't have any training for a decent job and, when times got hard, he found himself drifting without a dime, just walking and walking, while hope got dimmer with every sundown. Then, he came to our gate.

Jim, which was his name, stayed a good spell. Country air and good vittles, to say nothing of some good hard work in the fields, made a mighty big difference. He lost the cough he'd had when he came and his skin turned a decent tan. One day, standing with me by the barn he said, "This has to be about as close to heaven as I've ever been, maybe as close as I'll ever get." I allowed how it was right beautiful and that I hoped heaven had some meadows like ours. As for not getting any closer, well, we sat down on a bale of hay and talked about that.

I told Jim that almost all of us had been where he was in one way or another. Why, every one alive needs to find a place where he's needed and wanted and where there's work he can do. But more than all that, he needs to make friends with the Almighty, to learn about Jesus and His way of living and loving. When a person, man or woman, signs on with the Almighty's outfit, becomes one of His hands, he soon discovers all those other things, too!

Jim listened, looking sort of skeptical, and said something about how I should have been a preacher. I told him that I figured many a preacher should have been a cow poke and there's a cow poke or two who should have been preachers. As for me, I figure I'm just about where the Almighty wants me. The real question, though, was where He wanted Jim! Jim grinned and shook my hand. Before I let go we prayed, Jim putting the Almighty in charge of his life from then on, promising to follow Jesus as best he could.

That's all been awhile back now. Jim moved on and got himself a good job on a spread not far off. Last I heard he was getting married to some sweet little gal who loves ranching as much as Jim'd come to. I reckon it all goes to show you how the Almighty has a way of bringing folks together along the highways of His world. Me, I'm just mighty glad I could be there to open the gate when one of His strays came by.

ALWAYS
WATCHING

I was watching some colts
frisking in the pasture not long back while the mares
chomped grass, seeming to pay no mind to them but
watching pretty closely just the same. Set me to thinking
how things are with all of us.

I recall my own frisking days (as I suspect you to do,
too) and how my Ma used to keep her eye on me even
when it didn't seem she was noticing. But there came
times now and then when I'd up and do something
ornery. Then she'd spring into action real quick! It was
the same when danger or trouble came along; she was
there. And all she had to do was say the word and my
dad would be there too, snorting sparks and ready to
protect us.

I suppose it's that way with all God's creatures. Take
that pair of red-tail hawks that circle our valley. I wouldn't
want to put my hand into their nest and face their fury!
Almost all of God's creatures have the same instinct, to
watch over their own and sacrifice themselves, if need be,
to keep them safe.

Thinking about that makes it almost seem silly for us
to worry like we do, as though the Almighty would do
less, less than those two red-tails or a brood mare with

her colt. It just stands to reason, doesn't it? If God built that sort of caring into his creatures, man and beast alike, he's sure to have that same sort of caring himself. From what I read in the Good Book about Jesus, He must have figured that way too, seeing how that's what He taught. "You're worth more than a whole flock of sparrows," He said, "yet not one of them falls to the ground without your Heavenly Father knowing it."

But back to that frisking business. I don't reckon any of us get over it completely. Oh sure, we simmer down in some respects. But then we get ornery and clever to make up for it, like some horses do. But God just keeps caring, being patient, forgiving us and always trying to teach us better. If only we'd learn to obey when He touches the reins of our spirit or shifts His weight in the saddle of our conscience! Sure would save us a good deal of misery.

I figure that's why Jesus came, to show us how much the Almighty cares. I reckon one reason Jesus had to die was to show us what happens when folks don't learn the lessons of His loving, when they're strangers to God. But shucks, we don't *need* to be strangers, not with prayer so handy and Jesus to introduce us. And it's mighty comforting to know that, even if we should get lost in the badlands of life, even if a feller doesn't quite make it back...He's there. He'll see to it we find the Home Spread at last. He's watching even when it doesn't seem like it!

MOONLIGHT

I couldn't sleep last night somehow. I just lay there staring at the ceiling...thinking. "Well, Lord," I said, "guess you want to talk with me a spell. And if you do, I figure I'd better listen."

I pulled on my jeans and boots and moseyed out to that old stump in the pasture and sat down, gazing up at the moon. It was as big as a country pumpkin, making things almost as bright as day.

It struck me then how it was different a day or so back. A little bite appeared at one edge of that moon...kind of like a bite somebody's taken out of a biscuit. It kept getting bigger and bigger until there was hardly any light coming from that moon at all! Of course I knew what it was. We were having an eclipse. They say the moon hasn't got any light of its own—it just reflects the light of the sun. When this earth gets in between, its shadow falls on the moon and it stops shining.

I was pondering all this when it came to me. "That's what you wanted to tell me, Boss," I said. "I really don't have any light of my own either. I reckon the best a body can do is to try and reflect the light of Your Son and brighten things a bit for folks in these parts. But sometimes I let this world get in the way. . .and it casts a shadow on my life. I don't do much shining for you then. 'Eclipsed' I guess you'd say. . .because I let this old world get between me and Jesus. Of course, it shouldn't happen, but now and then it does. I need Your help, Boss, to see that it doesn't.

"I want to shine for You, Boss, in whatever time I got left down here. But as seasons come and go, I find myself looking beyond more than I used to. Someday I won't be around to shine down here. But I'll still be shining! Yep. I'll just be shining in another Heaven. Guess that's the one a fellow could call the real Home Spread."

I got up off that stump and smiled up at the moon, big as a country pumpkin and a whole lot brighter. "Guess that's what You wanted to tell me, Boss," I said. "Reckon I can get some shut-eye now." And I did.

BARNWOOD

A stranger came by the other day with an offer that set me to thinking. He wanted to buy the old barn that sits out by the highway. I told him right off he was crazy.

He was a city type. You could tell by his clothes, his car, his hands, and the way he talked. He said he was driving by and saw that beautiful barn sitting out in the tall grass and wanted to know if it was for sale. I told him he had a funny idea of beauty. Sure, it was a handsome building in its day. But then, there's been a lot of winters pass with their snow and ice and howling wind. The summer sun's beat down on that ole barn till all the paint's gone, and the wood has turned silver grey. Now the old

building leans a good deal, looking kind of tired. Yet, that fellow called it beautiful.

That set me to thinking. I walked out to the field and just stood there, gazing at that old barn. The stranger said he planned to use the lumber to line the walls of his den in a new country home he's building down the road. He said you couldn't get paint that beautiful. Only years of standing in the weather, bearing the storms and scorching sun, only that can produce beautiful barnwood.

It come to me then. We're a lot like that, you and I. Only it's on the inside that the beauty grows with us. Sure, we turn silver grey too. . .and lean a bit more than we did when we were young and full of sap. But the Good Lord knows what He's doing. And as the years pass He's busy using the hard weather of our lives, the dry spells and the stormy seasons, to do a job of beautifying in our souls that nothing else can produce. And to think how often folks holler because they want life easy!

They took the old barn down today and hauled it away to beautify a rich man's house. And I reckon some day you and I'll be hauled off to Heaven to take on whatever chores the Good Lord has for us on the Great Sky Ranch. And I suspect we'll be more beautiful then for the seasons we've been through here...and maybe even add a bit of beauty to our Father's house.

ILLUSTRATIONS BY CRIS MUSCOTT
DESIGNED BY LAURA HOUGH
TYPE SET IN PALATINO